WHERE
in the
WORLD
Are YOU?

What on Earth Books is an imprint of What on Earth Publishing
Allington Castle, Maidstone, Kent ME16 0NB, United Kingdom
30 Ridge Road Unit B, Greenbelt, Maryland, 20770, United States

First published in the United States in 2022

Written by Marie G. Rohde
Illustrated by Marie G. Rohde

Staff for this book: Nancy Feresten, Publisher; Laura Buller, Editorial
Director; Katy Lennon, Senior Editor; Andy Forshaw, Art Director;
Alenka Oblak, Head of Production.

With special thanks to Sophie Macintyre and Adriana Cloud.

ISBN: 9781913750763

DC/Foshan, China/03/2022
Printed in China

10 9 8 7 6 5 4 3 2 1

whatonearthbooks.com

WHERE in the WORLD Are YOU?

By **Marie G. Rohde**

What on Earth Books

Where is the cat?

Under the
wobbly table.

Where is the wobbly table?

On the blue rug.

Where is the blue rug?

In the yellow room.

Where is the yellow room?

Behind the
green door.

Where is the green door?

In the colorful apartment.

Where is the colorful apartment?

In the
pink house.

Where is the pink house?

On the
cheerful street.

Where is the cheerful street?

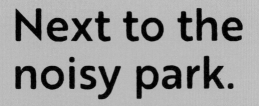

Next to the
noisy park.

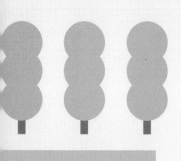

Where is the noisy park?

In the busy neighborhood.

Where is the busy neighborhood?

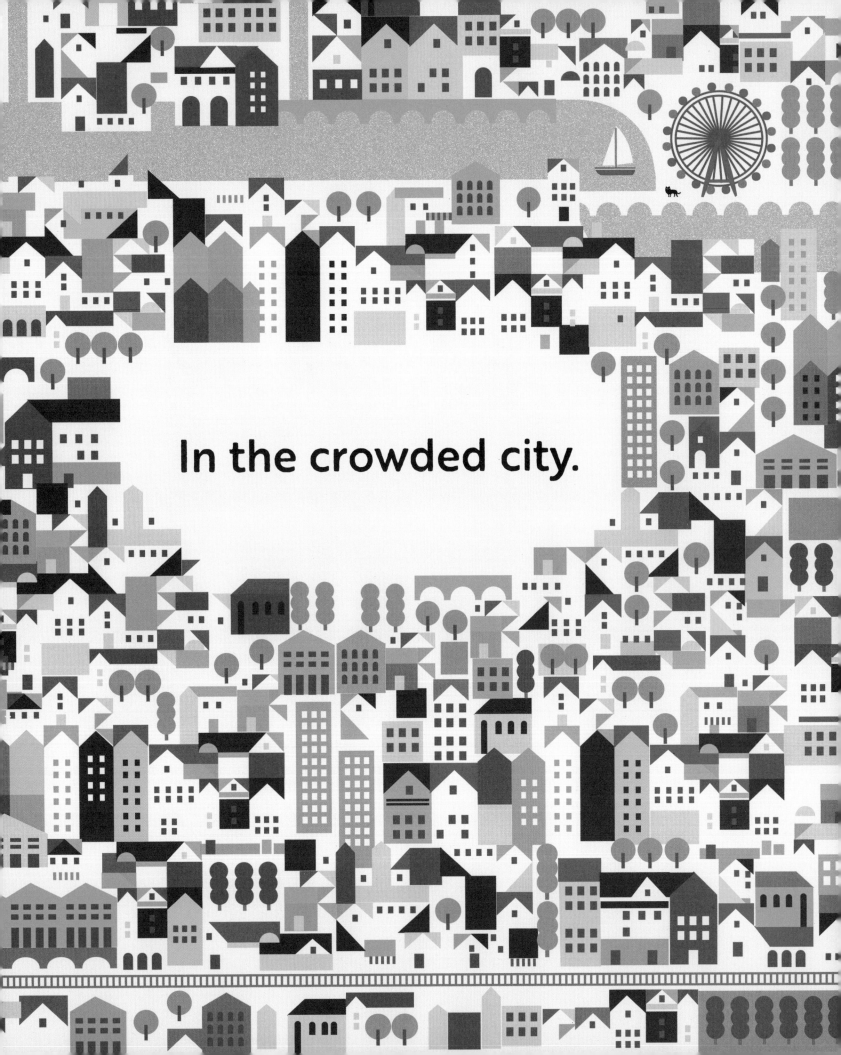

In the crowded city.

Where is the crowded city?

In the big
country.

Where is the big country?

On the vast continent.

Where is the vast continent?

Next to the
wide ocean.

Where is the wide ocean?

On the planet Earth.

Where is the planet Earth?

Spinning around the scorching Sun.

Where is the scorching Sun?

Among the
twinkling stars.

Where are the twinkling stars?

In our galaxy, the Milky Way.

Where is the Milky Way?

In the expanding universe.

Where is the expanding universe?

Here.

Here.

And here.
It's everywhere!

Including . . .

under the
wobbly table.

The cat is . . .

Under the **wobbly table**,
on the blue **rug**,
in the yellow **room**,
behind the green **door**,
in the colorful **apartment**,

in the pink **house**,
on the **cheerful street**,
next to the **noisy park**,
in the **busy neighborhood**,
in the **crowded city**,

in the **big country**,
on the **vast continent**,
next to the **wide ocean**,
on the **planet Earth**,
spinning around the **scorching Sun**,

among the **twinkling stars**,
in our galaxy, **the Milky Way**,
in the **expanding universe**!

Now,
where are YOU?

The story behind this book

Children were not allowed out in the street during the first strict Covid-19 lockdown here in Spain in 2020. During this time, my son was being homeschooled like many other children, and was invited to participate in a group storytelling activity. His story started simply: "Where is the shopping basket?" And gradually it zoomed out from our home, connecting us with the prohibited world outside.

I liked it so much that I started to make an illustrated version. Along the way, a black cat, awfully similar to my grandmother's mischievous cat Timmy, appeared in the story.

You wouldn't have it in your hands without the original idea from my son Valeri, the cheerful support and ideas from my partner Roger and my editor Katy, and the creative and thoughtful art direction from Andy.

I have always been a creative person, ever since growing up in Sweden, where I was surrounded by books in various languages, beautiful fabrics, and art materials.

After moving to Barcelona, Spain, to study Architecture, I started a blog about the fortunes and misfortunes of finding your way in a foreign city. My blog gathered a dedicated following and opened up many doors for me. Eventually I began to receive commissions for illustration and print design work.

Some years ago, several of my interests came together in my first book, *Planet SOS*. It has been published in 14 languages and selected by the United Nations' Sustainable Development book club. I look forward to writing and illustrating many more books in the future. *Where in the World Are You?* is my second book.